1950

1955

1976

1989

1999

1949

1970

1979

1992

UNIVERSITY OF MARYLAND TRADITIONS
First Edition
August 2011

DISCLAIMER
Although we, the authors, have made every effort to make certain that all the information in this book was correct at press time, we do not assume and hereby disclaim any liability to any party for any loss, damage, or disruption caused by errors or omissions, whether such errors or omissions result from negligence, accident, or any other cause. Never fear! We'll clear them all up in the second edition!

CREDITS
Cover Photograph Copyright © 2011 by John T. Consoli, University of Maryland

Book design and production by LMH Design Associates, LLC

ACKNOWLEDGEMENTS
The most fantastic photographer in the world: John T. Consoli
The ever faithful University Archives staff
Doug Dull from University of Maryland Athletics
Michael Fribush, Maryland Media Inc. (Step Show photos, page 25)

And a special shout out to UMD student David Nelson '11, who worked tirelessly on the University of Maryland Traditions Initiative during his four years at Maryland. Dave wrote the "Terp Talk" section of this book. He was one of our inspirations! Go Dave!

ISBN: 978-0-615-52272-2

MARYLAND

1920 turtle power

Tradi

THE LAST NOTES OF THE BAND DIE AWAY…out of the Comcast Center flows a throng of people. Between the brilliance of gleaming whites and flashing colors…a number of figures dressed in solemn black stand out…beneath the dignity of their mortar boards, we see their faces…some bewildered, others laughing, self-assured…members of the Class of Years Gone By.

Wow! Where DID the time go? That's what they're asking themselves. Attending classes, going to games, traveling on alternative spring breaks or study abroad…many memories to take away, huh? And…an awesome education. They earned their way to graduation by more than applying themselves to studies: they wove themselves into the fabric of the University of Maryland.

And, more than likely they didn't even realize that was happening. It probably began when they got used to the "ways of Maryland"…when

tions

they started texting "my school," "my Terps," "my Maryland Marching Band," "my favorite professor"…when they learned the Maryland lingo…like saying, "the Stamp" (Stamp Student Union)…or knowing that "the Beast" is CRS's climbing wall, or that other "Wall" in the Comcast Center…they were weaving themselves into Maryland. And now they are leaving behind that part that they have given.

Someday that will be you…beneath the dignity of your mortar boards, and we will see your faces…some of them bewildered, others laughing, self-assured…members of the Class of _____ …and you, too, will

INSERT YOUR CLASS YEAR HERE

have become part of the tradition that is the University of Maryland.

By the way…do you know all the words to the "Maryland Victory Song"? And what if someone asks you what a Terrapin is or "how do I get to the Dairy for some ice cream?" I'm just saying…

...the University of Maryland gets into your soul, and it's one of those places where a piece of your heart will always remain.

DYK: There are 650 acres that encompass the main campus, not including the woods and the golf course.

turtle love

Blast from the Past

HISTORY SNAPSHOT: March 6, 1856, the Maryland General Assembly chartered a new institution of higher education, the Maryland Agricultural College. Three years later, Oct. 5, 1859, the doors were thrown open to the first students—eager to learn about agriculture and engineering.

Through the years, the Maryland Agricultural College grew into the Maryland State College, and finally, the University of Maryland. Today, as the flagship of the state's 12-campus university system, UMD counts more than 2,800 faculty members who teach 25,000 undergraduate students and nearly 10,000 graduate students. There are over 100 majors to choose from, and the university is now one of the nation's top 20 public research universities and an economic catalyst for the state.

Would you believe that Maryland's 150-year history includes many tra-

DYK: There are 270 buildings on campus.

Creepy! On November 29, 1912 around 10:30 p.m., a fire broke out in the attic of the newest administration building where a Thanksgiving dance was being held. Fanned by a strong southwest wind, the fire destroyed the barracks where the students were housed, all the school's records, and most of the academic buildings, leaving only Morrill Hall untouched. Okay. Now comes the creepy part: a large brick and concrete compass inlaid in the ground before the fire designates the former center of campus as it existed in 1912. Lines engraved in the compass point to each building that was destroyed in the Thanksgiving Day fire. The only building not marked on the compass is Morrill Hall, which was eerily spared by the blaze. Creepy!

Is this a turtle race?

Class wars

The annual tug-of-war between the freshman and sophomore classes during the spring semester marked the end of the beanie-wearing season for freshmen. Roll the video tape: freshmen on one side of the banks of Paint Branch Creek...sophomores on the other...planting their feet and pulling that rope! This traditional contest started around 1915, and continued into the early 1950s.

ROBERT JOHNSTON McCUTCHEON, I. S.
Braddock, Md.

ditions that date back to the early days of the Maryland Agricultural College, including "class wars?" Harken (like that word, harken?) yourself back to the days in the early part of this century when competitions involved first- and second-year students playing King of the Mountain on a 120-foot iron water tower located on campus. This hair-raising tradition continued until 1913 when wily sophomore Robert McCutcheon (over there on the left) knocked down the freshman flag with a well-placed rifle volley to its staff. Come ooo-on!

And, we really can't forget about those freshmen beanies…From the 1920s to the 1960s, freshmen students were required to wear beanies everywhere they went on campus, from their first day of school until the freshmen-sophomore tug-of-war, held during the spring semester. The beanies were known as "rat caps" for the men, and "rabbit caps" for the women…more about that later.

So, tighten your seat belt and hold on to your chair… you're about to meet your University of Maryland traditions!

BOO OF THE WEEK:
Starting in the 1920s, and continuing for nearly 40 years, the university required freshmen to wear beanies everywhere they went on campus...from their first day of school until the freshman-sophomore tug-of-war. The beanies were called "rat caps" for the men and "rabbit caps" for the women. Imagine walking out of your dorm to your first class at UMD with a "rat cap" or "rabbit cap" on your head!

rabbit cap

Traditional Songs

Alma Mater

Hail, Alma Mater!
Hail to thee Maryland!
Steadfast in loyalty,
For thee we stand.
Love for the black and gold,
Deep in our hearts we hold.
Singing thy praise forever,
Throughout the land.

Maryland Victory Song

Maryland, we're all behind you,

Raise high the black and gold.

For there is nothing half so glorious,

As to see our team victorious.

We've got the steam boys,

We've got the team boys,

So keep on fighting, don't give in!

M-A-R-Y-L-A-N-D (yell)

Maryland will win!

Words and music by Thornton W. Allen
Copyright 1928 by the Student Assembly of Maryland

Fight Song

Fight, fight, fight for Maryland,

Honor now her name again,

Push up the score, keep on fighting for more,

For Maryland, GO TERPS!

And we will fight, fight, fight for terrapins,

Keep on fighting 'til we win.

So sing out our song as we go marching along,

To victory!

Words and music by Ralph Davis '41
Copyright 1941 by the University of Maryland
Student Government Association

Yells!

Hee — Haw — Ho — Go

Mar — y — land

Hee — Haw — Ho — Go

Mar — y — land

Hee! Haw! Ho! Go! Maryland

Hee! Haw! Ho! Go! Maryland

From the 1926 *Reveille* yearbook

"red"

Oh, so you're THAT Maryland fan! The one who won't wear any colors except red and white… especially on game day…and certainly not blue and gold. You love your Maryland sports, and are a devoted Terp…one who never turns off the TV when the Terps are playing…and you're always ready for the Red-White Spring Football Game or Midnight Madness. You put your UMD passion front and center, whether you're watching the Terps in the Orange Bowl, cheering on our championship basketball teams, or supporting Maryland's world-class soccer, field hockey or lacrosse teams. You're that fan that shows everyone which team rocks the ACC. **Go Terps!**

Shake it,
shake it, baby

At home basketball games, UMD students vigorously shake campus newspapers while pretending to read them as the visiting team is being introduced.

We won't mention some of the other, ahem, "traditions!" that happen as the opposing team is introduced.

It's all about Gary...land

Gary Williams traditionally began every home game with his classic fist pumping action for the Maryland fans. After 22 years of coaching at his Alma Mater, he retired in 2011. He will continue to serve as an ambassador for the university.

For the record...

During his years at UMD, Gary Williams:

- Won 668 games, 461 at home;

- Won the 2002 NCAA National Championship;

- Led the Terps to 14 NCAA tournaments;

- Walked away with three ACC regular-season titles;

- Appeared in seven Sweet 16 games, two Elite Eights and two Final Fours;

- Was named national coach of the year in 2002 and the ACC coach of the year in 2002 and 2010.

tailgating

There's no better place to be.

On the menu:

• A beautiful fall day

• Homecoming Parade

• Tailgating in Lot 1 with 50,000 of your closest old friends

• Terps football on Capital One Field at Byrd Stadium.

Here we go Maryland...

Harry Clifton "Curley" Byrd was a lot of things at UMD...he was a student who graduated in engineering in 1905. In 1908, he began a 43-year career that included coaching the University of Maryland football team, teaching English and history, overseeing athletics as athletics director, and eventually becoming president.

During his tenure as president, Maryland became one of the largest universities in the country.

First football team 1892

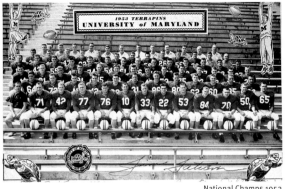

National Champs 1953

FOOTBALL FACTOIDS: Many Maryland players have received All-American honors. Eleven Terps have been named consensus (received a majority of votes) first-team All-Americans, and one, E.J. Henderson, has received that honor twice! Don't act too surprised when you learn that some have won prestigious awards, including the Bednarik Award, Butkus Award, Outland Trophy, and Lombardi Award. They are our Terps, after all!

DYK: Bob Pellegrini, Gary Collins, Randy White, and Boomer Esiason all finished in the top-ten of the voting for a Heisman Trophy.

RESPECT THE SHELL: Six Maryland players and four coaches have been inducted into the College Football Hall of Fame. Bear Bryant, Jerry Claiborne, Clark Shaughnessy, and Jim Tatum were inducted as coaches. These players...Dick Modzelewski, Bob Pellegrini, Jack Scarbath, and Bob Ward. Stan Jones and Randy White were also inducted into the Pro Football Hall of Fame.

Kevin Plank

WOW: Gymkana, founded at UMD in 1946, is one of the oldest groups of its kind in the United States.

66 One of my clearest memories of college is my strength coach at Maryland saying, 'Plank, stop worrying about all this other [business] crap and just commit yourself to playing football. You have the rest of your life to do these other things.' But I could never stop. I remember thinking how much fun it would be just to sit at a desk and think, 'All right, how are we going to make a buck?'" Kevin Plank, CEO and Founder of Under Armour

Then &

1951

The **Administration Building** is the center of campus life, socially, academically, and geographically.

Dedication of the stadium Many, many years ago when the Maryland football team was just beginning to develop, people began to dream. In those dreams of long ago, students saw themselves sitting in good seats at a football game, instead of in the hard bleachers of the end zone. They saw their parents and friends, too, being provided for. The dream was finally realized as the new Byrd Stadium was dedicated in a renewal of the ancient Navy-Maryland rivalry.

Homecoming As the Maryland alumni filed into the stadium, many for the first time, the main feature of the Homecoming Day began to unfold. For the first time in its history, the AFROTC marched en masse to a Maryland football game to watch, cheer and hope for a successful game.

HOLY COW! These traditions have been around a long time.

Then

1984

The **Stamp Student Union** is the center of campus life, socially, academically, and geographically.

Homecoming The celebration began on a Wednesday in October and lasted until late Saturday night. The theme was "A Cause for Celebration"...and celebrate they did. The festivities started with the theme decorations contest on the first day. Terp Talent night was Thursday. Homecoming Parade on Friday. Saturday began with a win over UNC, 44–21, and ended with the Homecoming Dinner Dance!

Commencement Those who graduated from the university on May 24, 1984, received the "personal touch." Each of the 3,650 grads were recognized individually as they received their diplomas. The commencement ceremonies, usually held in Cole Field House, were divided into 11 separate "mini-commencements," held in six buildings at three different times.

STEPPIN' OUT! Possibly the most anticipated tradition for Homecoming Weekend 1984 was the Annual Greek Step Show (right) sponsored by the Pan-Hellenic Council. Students dressed in their colors... stood in the spotlights stepping, ranking, dancing and singing their routines. They definitely rocked a packed Ritchie Coliseum.

1917 MARCHING BAND

THEY WILL ROCK YOU

THE MIGHTY SOUND OF MARYLAND

REGISTRATION

then

1953 With the opening of the fall semester came the inevitable registration week with all its confusion...and frustrations. Some lines seemed never ending; many nerves were shattered, yet, eventually everyone completed his or her schedule, paid his or her bill and rushed out to enjoy the next activity on the list of orientation week!

2011 Students register online while having a latte at Starbucks using their own computer or a cellphone.

DYK: Enrollment of first entering class of 1859 consisted of 34 male students.

& now

Byrd Beach

This is where you see it all, and we do mean all: students greeting the return of springtime warmth to the campus by donning their bathing suits and stretching out along the bleachers in Byrd Stadium to study, tan, and people watch. What more could one person want?

The Outdoor Aquatic Center opens in mid-April and closes in mid-October. It's always a cool 82 degrees. And don't forget the splash pool or the beach volleyball!

Eppley Rec Center

beach volleyball

I scream…you scream… we all scream for ice cream …from the Dairy

Maryland's ice cream tradition has been part of the school since 1924…that's more than 80 years!

The Dairy has been the favorite ice cream stop for many students over the years. Today, thousands of scoops are still dished out to customers of all ages. Many alums return…with their kids…to reminisce about the Dairy and its ice cream when they tour the campus.

Terps football lineman Randy White on a date at the Dairy in the 1970s.

DYK: The Dairy was originally nicknamed "The Shirt Factory" because of its "industrial appearance."

Once you try the newest ice creams at the Dairy…Fear the Turtle • Midnight Madness • Final Exam Cram…you'll really be a Terp!

Does Bacchus, the Roman god of wine, who graces the Memorial Gateway at Rossborough Inn, know something ghost-related? Maybe he knows who that ghost is that haunts the Rossborough Inn!

Is Morrill Hall haunted?

Marie Mount loved Maryland so much she didn't want to leave—even in death. So legend has it, the first dean of the College of Home Economics stayed—ultimately to haunt a building named after her.

Ghosts of UMD's past:

There is a ghost in Marie Mount Hall who supposedly plays the piano on stormy nights in the hall named for her, and members of the Maryland Ghosts and Spirits Association detected the presence of several other spirits in Marie Mount Hall during an investigation in October 2002.

Larry Donnelly, a former Dining Services employee, spotted a female ghost in the Rossborough Inn in 1981, during renovations to the building. Several weeks later, a waiter at the Inn saw the same woman, dressed in yellow, as Donnelly had described.

Spirits have also been spotted in Morrill Hall, and ghosts are rumored to inhabit Easton Hall, the Stamp Student Union, H. J. Patterson Hall, and the Alpha Omicron Pi and Kappa Delta sorority houses.

Mascot Mania:
Testudo over the years

TESTUDO, the official mascot of the University of Maryland, has never been your ordinary diamondback terrapin.

He is the symbol for our campus and has been for over 60 years… watching over all of us in good times and bad. Believe me, this is hard work! Testudo has experienced firsthand the dangers of being a campus celebrity, but more about that in a minute.

Testudo got his start back in 1932, when then football coach Curley Byrd, in response to *The Diamondback's* (the school newspaper even back then) search for a new "official" mascot, recommended the diamondback terrapin. At the time, the terrapin, a turtle native to the Chesapeake Bay and Byrd's hometown of Crisfield, Md., seemed a logical choice. It also became the Maryland state reptile.

But more about the dangers of Testudo's celebrityness: In 1947 students from Johns Hopkins University stole the bronze statue of the mascot and returned with it to their campus in Baltimore. Maryland students went up to Baltimore to retrieve Testudo and ended up besieging the dorm where the Johns Hopkins students

Straight from our UMD Facebook fans:

HOW MANY TIMES YOU RUBBED TESTUDO'S NOSE FOR LUCK: AT LEAST 32,865,754,876,854 :) ONCE…FIRST DAY OF CLASSES! :) EVERY TIME I WALKED BY IT! :) MORE THAN I CAN COUNT. I

The 1933 Senior Class Gift was a perfect 500-pound reproduction of a diamondback terrapin. Pictured left to right at the unveiling of the first Testudo: President Raymond Pearson, Vice President Harry Clifton Byrd, and SGA President Ralph Williams.

were keeping him; over 200 riot police were called in.

Then, in 1949, President Byrd (yes, now he was president) was rousted out of bed by a phone call from a University of Virginia fraternity requesting that Testudo be removed from their lawn. Once Testudo got back on campus, he was filled with 700 pounds of cement and fastened to his pedestal to ensure that he would not be stolen again any time soon.

However, students at rival schools still vandalized him, and in the 1960s Testudo was moved from its location on Baltimore Avenue to a spot in front of McKeldin Library in the center of campus. It's there that Testudo remains, a good luck charm for students who rub his nose and leave him offerings during finals week. That's another tradition!

Testudo Gigantia? I don't know, but he's cute as shell!

Why our mascot was named Testudo is very mysterious. A serious contender for its name's origin is that it was derived from the scientific classification

for turtle, testudines. Another is that the name is from testudo gigantia, a species native to the African country, Seychelles, and the remote island Aldabra. Finally, the derivation of the word testudo itself comes from the Latin word for a protective shelter used for Roman soldiers' heads, similar to a tortoise shell. Is this TMI?

So, while Testudo continues to preside over our campus, legends still swirl around campus about our 1,000-pound mascot. In fact, many believe that rubbing his nose will bring good luck on exams (hence Testudo's unusually shiny nose). What have you got to lose?

wwtd?

what would Testu-do?

Traditionally, it's thought that offerings bring **good luck** from Testudo.

SHHHH...BIG SECRET: There are "echo spots," mysterious locations on campus mostly along the mall, that reflect the sound of voices. The most prominent echo spot is the podium inside a 4-foot circular wall in front of Montgomery Hall. Many of the echo spots, including the podium which was intended for a statue that was never made, were created in the mid-1980s as a part of landscaping efforts to improve drainage on the mall and deter people from walking on the grass. Other good echo spots are the alcoves along the mall and spaces in front of Holzapfel, Symons, Marie Mount, Woods, Tydings and H.J. Patterson halls facing the mall.

The "Kertle" statue (Kermit + Turtle...in case you don't get it!) was part of the University of Maryland's 150th Anniversary celebration in 2006.

Romancing the turtle

Tender-hearted traditions: engagements, fountain proposals, smooching, weddings

Your first trip to the "kissing tunnel" was meant to ensure love and luck at college.

In the 50s, all freshmen were reminded that a penny in the wishing well behind the Rossborough Inn was guaranteed to make one's fondest dreams come true!

When you're ready to do the Chapel of Love thing, Testudo says to do what lots of Terps have already done: Do it at the Memorial Chapel! In the past, couples had to wait in line, sometimes overnight, to get a preferred date the following year. The line of prospective couples formed before the reservations office even opened on the first of each month...many made it a romantic occasion with picnic baskets and lawn chairs. All that's changed now...you can reserve your spot online!

Dude, you've got to walk the walk and talk the talk.

Maryland students speak many languages, not the least of which is "Terp Tongue"… for seasoned Terps, things like the Graham Cracker, CSPAC, DOTS, and The Beast, roll right off their tongues. Never fear! You too, will learn Terp Tongue in no time at all!

huh?

ACC (Atlantic Coast Conference): The University of Maryland is a charter member of this intercollegiate athletics organization. The Terrapins compete against UVA, NC State, Georgia Tech, Clemson, FSU, UNC, Wake Forest, Duke, Virginia Tech, Miami, and Boston College in various sports.

The Acropolis: Look out for a circular memorial set into the sidewalk between Shoemaker and Lefrak Halls. It marks the spot of the Great Fire of 1912. The unevenly spaced lines converging in the center of the brick circle point to where buildings once stood. There is a tale that if a prospective student steps at the convergence of these lines, he or she will not be granted admission to the university. But, some people say that if a current student steps on this spot, he or she will not graduate from here! Who knows?

Art Attack: Art Attack is a yearly event held in May. Usually the largest concert event at the university. You'll find art and cultural displays, music, and, often, celebrity appearances.

Art/Soc (pronounced "Art Sosh"): Art-Sociology Building; home to the departments of Art and Sociology.

Baltimore Avenue (aka Route One): The main road passing through the city of College Park. Stores, restaurants, and various other businesses line this busy street.

The Beast (aka Climbing Wall): Rock your world at the rock climbing wall located behind the Eppley Recreation Center. It's the tallest of its kind in the nation.

Black & Gold: The original colors of the Maryland Agricultural College and two of the four official university colors. Black and gold are considered the academic colors of the university, while red and white are regarded as its athletic colors.

Book Exchange: University clothing/book store on Route One, across from South Gate.

BSOS (pronounced "Bee Sauce"): The College of Behavioral and Social Sciences. Home to two of the most popular majors at the university: Government & Politics and Economics.

Byrd Stadium: Constructed in 1950, Byrd Stadium (now known as Capital One Field at Byrd Stadium) was named for Harry Clifton Byrd, class of 1908 and president of the University of Maryland from 1935 to 1954. "Home of the Maryland Terrapins." This is where the football and lacrosse teams play.

Byrd Beach: Students greet the return of spring warmth by donning their bathing suits and stretching out along the bleachers in Byrd Stadium to study, tan, and people watch.

Chapel Chimes: Hourly toll of the bells that play the Alma Mater, Westminster Chimes, and an extensive library of pop songs.

Chapel Field (aka Chapel Lawn): The field located in front of Memorial Chapel. This is a popular place for year-around outdoor recreation and is where the Mighty Sound of Maryland rehearses each fall.

Chapel (aka Memorial Chapel): Dedicated on October 6, 1952, this iconic campus landmark is a non-denominational house of worship that stands as a lasting memorial to the men and women of the university who served in the United States military. It is used for many events and concerts throughout the year, including graduation ceremonies for some of the smaller colleges. It is the most popular place for Terps to tie the knot.

The Class of 1910 Gate: A commemorative wrought iron gate situated between Turner Hall and the Rossborough Inn on Baltimore Avenue.

Cole or Cole Field House: A storied indoor sports arena next to the Student Union. Before the Comcast Center was constructed, this field house was where the university held its indoor athletic events. The Terps defeated the University of Virginia in both the first (December 2, 1955) and last (March 3, 2002) games in Cole Field House. The first athletic event held between the United States and China was a table tennis tournament located inside Cole Field House. Legendary performers such as Elvis Presley, Aretha Franklin, and the Rolling Stones have performed here.

The Class of 1910 Gate

MEMORIZE THIS DATE:

1856

Comcast or Comcast Center: Home of the Maryland men's and women's basketball teams. Sometimes referred to as "The Shell." Comcast seats 17,950 Terps' fans and opened in the fall of 2002.

CSPAC (pronounced "see spack"): Dedicated in 2001, the 318,000 square-foot Clarice Smith Performing Arts Center, designed by Moore Ruble Yudell, is located on 17 acres at the northwest end of campus, and is the largest single building ever constructed by the State of Maryland.

The Dairy (aka Turner Hall): The Dairy building, constructed in 1924 and named for Philip C. Turner, a member of the Board of Regents, 1941–52. The best thing about the Dairy is it's famous ice cream! Get some...now!

DBK or D-Back or *The Diamond-back*: The university's award-winning, independent student newspaper. First published in 1909.

DOTS: You will learn what this acronym means the moment you step on campus...Department of Transportation Services. Don't look now, they're right behind you!

ERC (aka Eppley Recreation Center): Inside the ERC you find more fitness stuff than you can throw a weight bench at...it also includes an Outdoor Aquatic Center.

The Farm (aka Campus Farm): An on-campus, fully operating farm.

"Fear the Turtle": This is sure to become your rallying cry! It became extremely popular with the men's basketball team's 2001 trip to the NCAA Final Four. It's also of one of the five flavors of ice cream introduced at the Dairy in spring 2004.

Find the "M": Among the oldest representations of the "M" that still survive on campus are those on Ritchie Coliseum (shown, left) and Turner Hall.

Flagship: Get used to it...the University of Maryland, College Park, is the largest campus of the University System of Maryland, and the Maryland General Assembly officially designated it "the flagship campus" in 1988.

Founding Date: Okay...you should probably memorize this, too...the Maryland Agricultural College, as the University of Maryland was then known, received its charter from the Maryland General Assembly on March 6, 1856.

Founders' Gate (aka North Gate): No, this isn't the same as "Founding Date!" The northernmost (and main) entrance to the University of Maryland campus by way of Baltimore Avenue.

The Fountain (aka ODK Fountain, Omicron Delta Kappa Fountain): A multi-tiered fountain located at the heart of McKeldin Mall. The engraved names recognize members of one of the most prestigious honor societies on campus, the Omicron Delta Kappa National Leadership Honor Society.

The Four Circles: TMI, again... there are four traffic circles on campus. One is located near the main entrance of the university (known as the "M" Circle); one is located near the Art-Sociology Building/Hillel Jewish Community Center; one is located next to the Samuel Riggs IV Alumni Center; and one is located in front of the main entrance to the Clarice Smith Performing Arts Center.

Frat Row (aka Fraternity Row): Frat row was constructed between 1914 and 1963, and is home to of 14 of the campus's fraternity and sorority chapters. This site was used in the film "St. Elmo's Fire" starring Emilio Estevez.

Gatehouse: Located at the main (north) entrance to campus, the Gatehouse has four plaques honoring the founders of the Maryland Agricultural College; also featured at this gateway is a University of Maryland seal, gift of the Class of 1995.

Graham Cracker: Graham Cracker was the name given to the lot on

DYK: Fountains burble (is that really a word?) near the Riggs Alumni Center (above), Engineering Building, on Hornbake Plaza, Tawes Plaza, and McKeldin Mall.

Delta Mu Fraternity's Spring Dance at the Roosevelt Hotel in Washington, D.C., in 1927.

Meet Me at the "M" or The Floral "M": That would be the Circle "M" on Campus Drive with flowers in the shape of an "M." Flowers are planted twice a year...once in the fall with pansies and again in the spring with annuals, usually vodka begonias. It's the circle where lots of graduates have their photos taken after commencement.

DYK: Portions of the movie "St. Elmo's Fire," directed by Joel Schumacher, were filmed on campus in October 1984, and alumnus Redge Mahaffey also used the campus as a setting in his 1995 production "Life 101." The 2007 production "National Treasure: Book of Secrets," directed by Jon Turteltaub used McKeldin Mall and the Special Events Room in McKeldin Library as filming locations.

Maryland Basketball 1973–74: Len Elmore, Owen Brown, Lefty Driesell, Rich Porac, and Tom McMillen

College Avenue where pep rallies were held. It was first used from 1958 to 1963 when the lot was vacant, and the dirt-filled area looked like a "graham cracker." Get it?

The Hill (next to Stamp): A steep hill along the left side of the Student Union. Students find this a treacherous spot during inclement weather.

Hoff (aka The Hoff Theater): Hoff was constructed as part of the 1972 renovation of the Stamp Student Union, and was named for William Hoff, manager of the union, in 1975.

Hornbake or Hornbake Plaza: Hornbake was constructed in 1972 and named in 1980 for R. Lee Hornbake, professor of industrial education, dean of the faculty, and vice president for academic affairs. There are more books here than you can shake your backpack at...

"I'd Rather be Studying": The unofficial motto of the University of Maryland, as spoken by supposed university alumnus "Sarah Bellum."

The Kissing Tunnel or Bridge: A white bridge on Regents Drive next to Memorial Chapel. When the university student body was all male, the bridge marked the edge of campus. Students would smooch with their off-campus sweethearts under this bridge.

Knox Boxes (aka Knox Box Apartments): An off-campus housing option on Knox Road in College Park.

LaPlata Beach: An outdoor recreation facility consisting of volleyball and basketball courts and an Astroturf field.

Late Night: The South Campus Dining Hall and North Campus Diner's extended hours of operation. Students enjoy food not normally found on the day menu.

Lot One: Parking lot primarily for faculty. Students with cars on campus must apply for a Lot One Parking Permit, a coveted privilege. Lot One is considered by most to be the closest and most convenient parking option.

Lot Six: Parking lot primarily for undergraduate students with university-registered cars on campus. Located next to Comcast Center, this parking lot is the furthest from the center of campus and widely considered the most inconvenient parking option on campus.

The Mall or McKeldin Mall: The main hub of outdoor activity on campus. This area is a popular spot for recreation, relaxation, and university events. It is also the longest collegiate mall in the world.

Main Admin. or Main Administration: Main Administration Building; houses the Office of the President, Provost, Vice Presidents.

Mayer Mall: Uh, oh...it's another mall. What would a university be without more than one mall? This one stretches from Mowatt Road, passing Van Munching Hall, and up the hill toward the School of Architecture, Planning, and Preservation. It's named after Bill Mayer, who was a professor and Dean of the College of Business and Management.

Maryland Day: A yearly, all day campus-wide open house with more than 400 exhibits and activities scattered across campus.

McKeldin (aka McKeldin Library): The main university library. Constructed in 1958; named for Theodore R. McKeldin, governor of Maryland, 1951–59. As of April 2011, there were 1,872,417 volumes in McKeldin.

Maryland Madness: Charles "Lefty" Driesell, Maryland's men's basketball coach from 1969 to 1986, is generally credited with coining the term "Midnight Madness." Midnight Madness was created in 1970, when at midnight on the first official day of team practice, Coach Driesell had his players take laps around the track that used to encircle the field at Byrd Stadium.

The Mighty Sound of Maryland: The University of Maryland Marching Band; A 200+ member

Shuttle-UM

marching band that performs at every home football game and at least one away game each season. The band is famous for its signature moves, fast tempo, and original half-time show themes.

Morrill Quad (aka "The Yard): Morrill Quad is located in the middle of Tydings, Lefrak, Taliaferro, Shoemaker and Morrill residence halls, the last of which is the oldest building on campus. The historic quadrangle was once the mall of the original campus.

North Gate, 1920

"Night and Day:" This sculpture that resembles Stonehenge...you know...that place in England... is found along the path between Holzapfel and H. J. Patterson Halls. It was sculpted by Kenneth Campbell, art professor emeritus,

who taught stone carving for 15 years, and created in 1972. Just so you can sound "in the know," the pieces are said to represent the various stages of enlightenment.

NiteRide: A car escort service granted to students within a specified radius outside the campus.

North Campus: The northernmost section of campus, beginning at the north side of McKeldin Mall and extending to Comcast Center. It encompasses Denton, Ellicott, and Cambridge Communities.

North Gate (aka Founders' Gate): The northernmost (and main) entrance to the University of Maryland by way of Baltimore Avenue.

North Hill: A residence hall community on South Campus comprised of Anne Arundel, Caroline, Carroll, Dorchester, Queen Anne's, Somerset, St. Mary's, Wicomico, and Worchester Halls.

Nymburu (aka Nymburu Cultural Center): An intercultural community center adjacent to the Student Union. Nymburu was constructed in 1996...name means "Freedom House" in Swahili.

OIT (aka Office of Information Technology): A hot-spot whether registering for classes, accessing library or other sources of information, consulting online course syllabi, submitting a transcript request, or just checking the latest dining hall menu online. You'll find technology is integrated into nearly every facet of university life.

Paint Branch Creek: A small creek that runs through North Campus where, from 1915 until the early '50s, there used to be an annual struggle between the freshman and sophomore classes during the spring semester that marked the end of the beanie wearing season for the freshman

Peace Garden: This garden was created in 2003 to honor the memory of the victims of the September 11, 2001, terrorist attacks. The garden, located at the east end of McKeldin Mall near Main Administration, marks the spot where the flowers placed along the ODK fountain during the campus's memorial service on September 12, 2001, were buried. The site includes a plaque with the phrase "May Peace Prevail on Earth" and an explanation of the garden's origin.

Preinkert (aka Preinkert Field House): The cornerstone for Preinkert was laid June 8, 1931.

It is named for Alma H. Preinkert, registrar, from 1919–54.

Red and White (see Black and Gold): Maryland's official school colors are black, gold, red, and white, the colors of the Maryland state flag. This is a trick answer... or is it a question?

Riggs (aka Samuel Riggs IV Alumni Center): The center, right next to the stadium, is a monument to the achievements of alums.

Route One (aka Baltimore Avenue, U.S. Route 1): The main road through the city of College Park. Stores, restaurants, and various other businesses line this bustling street.

SGA: Student Government Association. Formed in 1919, this legislative body comprised of students works closely with university Administration to serve the campus community.

Shuttle-UM: Maryland's student-operated, free, campus bus service for students, faculty, and staff.

South Campus: The southernmost section of campus, beginning at the south side of McKeldin Mall, extends to Knox Road, encompasses South and North Hill, and South Campus Commons.

South Gate: The southernmost entrance to the University of Maryland campus by way of Baltimore Avenue.

Stamp (aka Student Union, Adele H. Stamp Student Union, Stamp Student Union): The main student resource center on campus. It's where you want to be for entertainment, eating, shopping, and getting involved with campus activities! Go there!

Sundial: The Sundial is located in the center of McKeldin Mall and was originally a gift from the Class of 1965, the Department of Physics and Astronomy, and friends of Professor Uco Van Wijk, who died in 1966. It has been renovated with donations from the Class of 1990.

Testudo: The name of the official mascot of the University of Maryland. Testudo became the university mascot in 1932, after Coach Harry "Curley" Byrd

recommended that the original mascot, "The Old Liners" be changed. There are six bronze statues of Testudo on campus, the most well known being the original, which is located in front of McKeldin Library. It is considered good luck to rub his nose. During exam week, students leave offerings for Testudo at the base of his pedestal. But, here's where it get complicated: You see, Testudo is a real mascot, too, who makes frequent appearances at most university events, sporting events, and even weddings!

Taliaferro Hall: A commonly mispronounced academic building on South Campus. Properly pronounced "Tolliver."

Tyser Tower: Tyser Tower was constructed in 1991 as the "Athletics Welcome Center" and press box in Byrd Stadium; 92 feet by 152 feet; named for Ralph J. Tyser, class of 1940 alumnus and major university supporter.

UBC (aka University Book Center): The official University of Maryland bookstore featuring Terp gear/clothing, text books and more...located in the basement of the Stamp.

The Wall: The largest of several student seating sections inside the Comcast Center. The section gets its name from the steep seating that extends from the court to the upper concourse, giving it the appearance of a "wall" of students.

Washington Quad: A scenic area on South Campus that is popular for recreation and relaxation. It is surrounded by Baltimore, Calvert, Frederick, Harford, Prince George's, and Washington residence halls.

The Yard (aka "Morrill Quad"): One of the oldest regions on campus. This scenic area is surrounded by Morrill, Tydings, Talliaferro, Shoemaker, and Lefrak Halls.

A whole lot of Terpness

TERP ALLEY: A street that runs from the Clarice Smith Performing Arts Center lawn, past the Alumni Center, and ends at the players' entrance to Byrd Stadium. Two and one half hours before each home game, fans line the Alley to watch the football team, led by the Mighty Sound of Maryland, make its way down Terp Alley and into Byrd Stadium.

TERP BUCKS: A dining option that permits students to use their I.D. to purchase food at various cafés and shops on campus.

TERPS: An abbreviated version of "Terrapins." Maryland athletes, as well as current and former students, are referred to as "Terps." A unifying cry that all Terps know is "GO TERPS!"

TERP ZONE: A late-night student activities center on the ground floor of the Student Union. Students may choose to go bowling, play billiards, or grab a bite to eat here.

TERRAPIN OR DIAMONDBACK TERRAPIN: The official mascot of the University of Maryland. A terrapin is a primarily aquatic species of turtle and a member of the family Emydidae. It is also the Maryland state reptile.

TERRAPIN COUNTRY: The affectionate name given to the University of Maryland community, both on campus and at large.

The Sundial on McKeldin Mall

QUIZ:

Can you name eight sculptures on campus? Close your eyes. NO PEEKING.

1. Henson Statue outside the Stamp Student Union dedicated to alumnus and Muppets' creator Jim Henson.

2. "Night and Day" sculpture resembling Stonehenge along the path between Holzapfel and H. J. Patterson Halls.

3. Untitled sculpture behind the Architecture Building, given in memory of Herbert E. Rycroft II, sculpted by Raymond Kaskey in 1972.

4. "Bradford," a metal sculpture in front of the Chemistry Building; created by Lila Katzen and given to the university by Lila and George Snow, professor of physics from 1958 to 1992.

5. Two glazed ceramic lions imported from China on either side of the doorway to the Institute for Global Chinese Affairs in Francis Scott Key Hall.

6. "Bird's I View" statue of a blue bird by Michele Colburn near Lot 1; it was originally sponsored by the Prince George's Arts Council.

7. Bust of Charles E. White in the Chemistry Library; White was professor of chemistry from 1938 to 1968 and department chair in 1966 and 1967; he was professor emeritus from 1968 to 1973; the Chemistry Library is named for him.

8. Bust of Glenn L. Martin in Glenn L. Martin Hall.

The more things change, the more they stay the same…

"Take Maryland as your mixing bowl and place therein approximately 10 thousand students, a few hundred faculty members, and assorted deans and advisors. Mix thoroughly with classrooms, text books, lectures and mud. Add football games, frat parties, tray rides, and class proms for spice; then stir in the rush of classes, a lack of sleep, tired looks, and a thriving No-Doz business. Shake up for finals and allow to sit for one week. For flavor, toss in one kissing tunnel, a serenade, and two people in love. Add a dash of ambition, a taste of self-management, and a whiff of the future. After sprinkling of snow and rain over all, allow to age slowly for four years. Top with a few crushed hopes for maturity, and serve on a white columned campus. What is it, you ask? Why it's MARYLAND!" —1959 UMD Yearbook

DYK: Willow oaks—69 of these trees line McKeldin Mall. (2004)

Special Days

Whew…Maryland definitely has had some SPECIAL (TIC*) days!

Way back when, one of the biggest "special days" was called May Day. Adele Stamp, UMD's first dean of women (1922–60) established the tradition of celebrating May Day in 1923. Stamp believed in providing activities that honored and celebrated women and their achievements. May Day provided just such an opportunity.

A May Queen was chosen from among the women of the senior class by votes cast by the junior women, and was to be selected based not on beauty alone, but upon "citizenship, scholarship and service to the university."

Activities featured female students ceremoniously dancing around the May pole, Mortar Board tapping, and…get ready now…crowning the May Day Queen!

Your typical May Day in the 1940s or 1950s: First came the welcome address given by Dean Stamp, followed by a lengthy procession lead by two junior ushers, followed by a junior representative of each dorm or sorority, followed by pages, followed by the honor guard of senior women. Well, you get the idea.

Once the honor guard was in place, the Queen (the first May Day Queen was Zita Enzer) and her court processed onto the green, sort of like a

*Tongue-in-Cheeky

wedding procession. The queen's entourage included flower girls, a crown bearer, a book bearer, and a train bearer. The book bearer presented a first-edition Terrapin yearbook to the Queen.

May Day would have also included songs, a pageant or play to honor the Queen, and the May pole dance. The last May Day was held in 1961.

In a handwritten piece concerning past May Days, Dean Stamp expressed her hope that the tradition would continue. "May Days were held at the university for 39 years. It may happen that in the years to come that May Day may be revived in a different form," she wrote.

And then there was Maryland Day! A recent tradition, it has been going strong since April 2000. It's now one of the top annual events in the state of Maryland. The university welcomes the entire Washington, D.C., region to have fun, learn and explore the UMD world.

Now part of Maryland Day, Ag Day has been a University of Maryland tradition since 1924...except for one year during World War II. In the 1920s, the Livestock Club held the first student-run fitting and showing contest, which was sponsored by the university. From demonstrations to landscape advice to ice cream tasting, Ag Day has something for everyone.

WOW: There are 12 colleges and schools on campus. Can you name them?

COLLEGE OF AGRICULTURE AND NATURAL RESOURCES; SCHOOL OF ARCHITECTURE, PLANNING, AND PRESERVATION; COLLEGE OF ARTS AND HUMANITIES; COLLEGE OF BEHAVIORAL AND SOCIAL SCIENCES; ROBERT H. SMITH SCHOOL OF BUSINESS; COLLEGE OF COMPUTER, MATHEMATICAL, AND NATURAL SCIENCES; COLLEGE OF EDUCATION; A. JAMES CLARK SCHOOL OF ENGINEERING; PHILIP MERRILL COLLEGE OF JOURNALISM; COLLEGE OF INFORMATION STUDIES; SCHOOL OF PUBLIC HEALTH; SCHOOL OF PUBLIC POLICY

UMD TRADITIONS | 58

Art Attack

Art Attack, a celebration of campus diversity through art and music, was founded in 1984 by University of Maryland student Keith Baltimore. Art Attack brings Maryland's many cultures together.

Popular Art Attack appearances include...All-American Rejects | Black Eyed Peas | Bloodhound Gang | The Bravery | Jackson Browne | George Clinton and the P-Funk All Stars | Chevelle | Cobra Starship | Common | Ben Folds | Gin Blossoms | Guster | Wyclef Jean | Ludacris | Ziggy Marley | Medicine | Moth | Outkast | Simple Plan | Spaz Band | Spill Canvas | Spine Of A Dog | Stryder | Sugar Ray | Timmy Tucker | Weezer | Zebrahead |

First Look Fair

Here's another interesting detail: First Look Fair is one of the longest running community traditions at the University of Maryland…going strong for 27 years! The annual event hosts more than 500 student clubs and organizations, campus departments and services, local vendors, and community service agencies. The festive atmosphere is the perfect place for students to learn more about how to get involved and connect with other students with similar interests. It's always a fantastic opportunity to discover everything that UMD has to offer!

Move-In Day

1951

Miss Marian Johnson is in charge of on- and off-campus housing for women. Don't you just love the bobby sox...not to mention the hat box!

 **2010**   New students are golf-carted…
some with their parents in tow…
to their new living quarters.

UMD VITS*

Brin, Sergey. The world's favorite search engine is home page for many a Web browser these days. And we all have Maryland alum Sergey Brin to thank for it. After graduating in 1993 with a B.A. in math and computer science, Brin headed to Stanford for graduate work. Brin was named Maryland's Outstanding Young Alumnus in May 2003, and was the winter 2003 commencement keynote speaker at the Comcast Center.

Calvert, Charles Benedict (1808–64). Central figure in the founding of the Maryland Agricultural College, president of the Board of Trustees, and well-known philanthropist, planter, and congressman; served as acting president, 1859–60.

Chung, Connie. American journalist. Connie Chung, who graduated from UMD in 1969, forged new territory in network news and broadcast journalism. As the first Asian American and second woman to be a news anchor, Chung has earned many awards for her work, including three Emmys.

Kennedy, John F. Sen. John F. Kennedy visited campus twice before he became president of the United States. His first visit was on April 27, 1959, when he was the featured speaker at spring convocation; speaking to a crowd of over 5,000, he encouraged the students to consider entering politics and to work to solve the problems of the

*Very Important Terps

Henson, Jim. He graduated from the University of Maryland in 1960, and is known the world over for his creation of the Muppets and his work in television with "Sesame Street" and "The Muppet Show." His work on film included seven movies starring the Muppets and two fantasy pieces, "The Dark Crystal" and "Labyrinth."

Olympians

A number of athletes from UMD have participated in the Olympics, including:

- Desmond Armstrong, 1998 and 1992, men's soccer
- Vicky Bullett, 1988 (gold medalist) and 1992 (bronze medalist), basketball
- Danny Califf, 2000, men's soccer
- Kem Clark, 1948, canoeing
- Carin Cone, 1956, (Australian silver medalist), 100-meter backstroke
- Mark Coogan, 1996, marathon
- Arthur E. Cook, Jr., 1948 (gold medalist), shooting
- Dominique Dawes, 1996 (bronze medalist in floor exercise and gold medalist in team all-around) and 2000, gymnastics
- John Eiseman, 1948, canoeing
- Ernie Fisher, 1956, wrestling
- Paula Girven, 1976, high jumping
- Lea Hakala, 1984, basketball (Finnish team)
- Erika Hansen, 1988 and 1992, swimming
- Tara Heiss, 1980, basketball
- Kelli Hill, 2000 and 2004, gymnastics (head coach)
- Tom Horton, 1948, canoeing
- Sarunas Jasikevicius, 2000 (bronze medalist) and 2004, men's basketball (Lithuanian team)
- Katie Kauffman-Beach, 1996, field hockey
- Kris Kirchner, 1980, basketball
- Irene Knox, 1932, shooting
- Howard B. Labow, 2000, fencing coach (Israeli team)
- John Maddocks, 1984, sailing (British team)
- Kerry McCoy, 2000 and 2004, wrestling
- Tom McMillen, 1972 (silver medalist), basketball
- Missy Meharg, 1996, field hockey (coach)
- Renaldo Nehemiah, 1980, track
- Jasmina Perazic, 1984, basketball (Yugoslavian team)
- Lauren Powley, 2008, field hockey
- Dina Rizzo, 2008, field hockey
- Steve Sheppard, 1976 (gold medalist), basketball
- Sara Silvetti, 2008, field hockey (alternate)
- Keli Smith, 2008 field hockey
- Todd Sweeris, 1996 and 2000, table tennis
- Andrew Valmon, 1988 (gold medalist) and 1992 (gold medalist), track
- Charles "Buck" Williams, 1980, basketball

Olympian Dominique Dawes

UMD President Wilson Elkins and Queen Elizabeth II at Byrd Stadium

nation. A little more than a year later, Sen. Kennedy was back at the University of Maryland, on May 14, 1960, to attend a rally supporting his campaign for the presidency.

Plank, Kevin. (See page 23.)

Everybody knows the story about how Kevin Plank was the self-proclaimed sweatiest guy on the football team when he played for UMD. He was determined to find a material that would wick to keep him dry and comfortable. He ran through seven prototypes before settling on the one he would use. Under Armour was born. Kevin is a long-time supporter of the Robert H. Smith School of Business and is responsible for the annual Cupid's Cup business competition, which has become a tradition in its own right at Maryland.

Presidents

The first president to visit campus was Dwight D. Eisenhower. Lyndon Johnson paid a surprise visit when he decided at the last moment to address a conference taking place on campus on October 15, 1966. Bill Clinton visited campus in 1993 to celebrate the Summer of Service program, and again in 1999, to advocate for more support for the Americorps program. Jimmy Carter gave the 2nd Annual Sadat Lecture for Peace on October 25, 1998. President Barack Obama spoke to a rally in support of his health care proposal on September 17, 2009, and most recently held a Town Hall Meeting at UMD on July 22, 2011.

Presley, Elvis.

Presley performed two concerts in Cole Field House, on September 27 and 28, 1974, to packed houses. Elvis is also connected to campus through Jack R. Salamanca, professor of English, author of the novel "The Lost Country." Salamanca's work was the basis for Elvis's film "Wild in the Country," which originally appeared in 1961.

Queen's Game

Queen Elizabeth II and her husband, Prince Philip, visited Byrd Stadium on October 19, 1957, to see "a typical American sport." As guests of then university President Wilson H. Elkins and Maryland Gov. Theodore R. McKeldin, they watched the Terrapins defeat the University of North Carolina Tar Heels 21 to 7. This major upset of one of the Terps' fiercest rivals has become known as the "Queen's Game."

Resnik, Judith.

Resnik graduated from the University of Maryland in 1977 with a Ph.D. in electrical engineering. She was the second American woman astronaut to orbit the earth on the space shuttle Discovery in 1984. A mission specialist for the space shuttle Challenger, Ms. Resnik died when the shuttle exploded in 1986.

Tydings, Joseph.

Tydings was president (aka prexie) of the Student Government Association in 1950 and graduated from the University of Maryland School of Law in 1953. Tydings was elected as a Democrat to the United States Senate in 1964. While senator, he was the chairman of the Committee on the District of Columbia in the 91st Congress. His father, Millard Tydings, also a U.S. senator from Maryland, graduated from the Maryland Agricultural College in 1910. Tydings Hall on campus is named for him.

Weinermobile

2001 graduate LaToya Morgan (left) is the first Terrapin known to have driven the Oscar Mayer company's 27-foot-long Weinermobile. Morgan, a communications major, who was on the road with the Weinermobile from summer 2001 to summer 2002, traveled an average of 500 miles per week!

Judith Resnik

Joseph Tydings

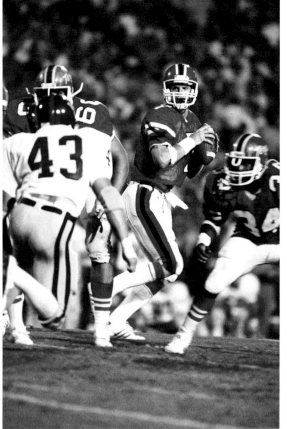
"Boomer" Esiason

DYK: The Terrapins have sent 14 quarterbacks to the National Football League: Bob Avellini, Jim Corcoran, Norman "Boomer" Esiason (above), Stan Gelbaugh, Shaun Hill, Mark Manges, Scott Milanovich, Tommy Mont, Neil O'Donnell, Al Pastrana, Frank Reich, Jack Scarbath, Dick Shiner, and Scott Zolak, earning the university the nickname "Quarterback Factory."

THE FINAL FOUR: Things to Do Before You Leave

Men's basketball national championship team 2002: Let the tradition begin.

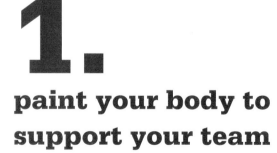

1.

paint your body to support your team

2.

**rub Testudo's nose
for good luck**

4.
pay those *#@!#* parking tickets

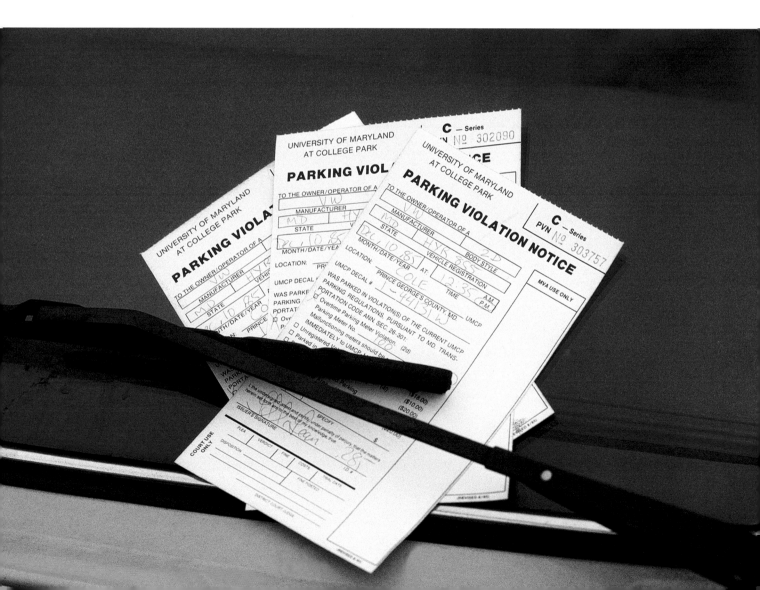

And now, our story's told,

Our pathway has been made;
It winds and twists behind us,
Through sunshine and through shade.

Let us reflect the days
That made us friends most true;
When health, and joy, and wealth,
Each classmate wished for you.

And on into the world,
Of strife which we must bear,
Let's think of _____,
INSERT YOUR CLASS YEAR HERE
And fight each battle Fair.

Forget the times we've erred,
Create a Perfect Day;
Dispel the clouds of doubt,
Spread sunshine in the way.

—H.B. Derrick, President of the Class of 1917

This University of Maryland Traditions book was
brought to you by UMD and:

Margaret and Boomer

Linda and Kermit

Linda Martin and **Margaret Hall**, both
UMD grads, have enjoyed working for the University of
Maryland for more than 20 years. They are proud and loyal
Terps who take pride in sharing their unique (and somewhat
wacky) perspective on university traditions.

1933

1936

1939

1948

1944

1935

1942

1945